American Lives

Sally
Ride

Elizabeth Raum

Heinemann Library
Chicago, Illinois

© 2006 Heinemann Library
a division of Reed Elsevier Inc.
Chicago, Illinois

Customer Service 888-454-2279
Visit our website at www.heinemannlibrary.com

Designed by Joanna Hinton-Malivoire and
Q2A Creative

Printed in China by
WKT Company Limited

10 09 08 07 06
10 9 8 7 6 5 4 3 2 1

Library of Congress Cataloging-in-Publication Data
Raum, Elizabeth
Sally Ride / Elizabeth Raum.-- 1st ed.
   p. cm. -- (American lives)
   Includes bibliographical references and index.
   ISBN 1-4034-6941-5 (hc) -- ISBN 1-4034-6948-2
   (pb)
   1. Ride, Sally--Juvenile literature. 2. Women
astronauts--United States--Biography--Juvenile
literature. 3. Astronauts--United States--Biography--
Juvenile literature. I. Title. II. Series.
   TL789.85.R53R38 2005

   629.45'0092--dc22

                 2005006255

Acknowledgments
The author and publishers are grateful to the
following for permission to reproduce copyright
material: Associated Press pp. 15 (Ron Lindsey), 23
(David Pickoff), 28 (Denis Poroy); Children's Press,
Chicago pp. 6, 9; Corbis pp. 4, 8 (Tim Maguire), 10
(Bob Krist), 12, 16 (Roger Ressmeyer), 22; Corbis/
Bettmann cover, pp. 11, 19, 20, 21; Corbis/Reuters
p. 29; Lothrop, Lee & Shepherd Books p. 27; NASA
pp. 14, 18; NASA/Johnson Space Center title page,
pp. 5, 13, 17, 24, 25, 26

Every effort has been made to contact copyright
holders of any material reproduced in this book.
Any omissions will be rectified in subsequent
printings if notice is given to the publisher.

9/2014
T 384
$5.00
92 RID

The photograph on the cover is an official NASA
portrait of Sally Ride, taken on September 15, 1978.

Contents

Some words are shown in bold, **like this.** You can find out what they mean by looking in the glossary.

Ride, Sally Ride

On June 18, 1983, Dr. Sally Ride climbed inside the space shuttle *Challenger* and buckled her seat belt. She checked that her equipment was working, then she settled back and waited for launch. She was about to make history. Sally Ride would be the first American woman in space. She would also be the first astronaut to use a robot arm to move a **satellite** from space to the shuttle's **cargo bay.**

The seventh shuttle flight lifts off with Dr. Sally Ride on board.

Timeline

1951	1973	1978	1982	1983
Born in Los Angeles, California	***Graduates** from Stanford University*	*Selected for astronaut training*	*Marries Steven Hawley*	*First shuttle mission*

Sally Ride was the first American woman in space.

Sally Ride was not the only one excited about her trip into space. Over 250,000 people stood on the nearby Florida beaches and watched the launch of the *Challenger* that morning. Some wore T-shirts that said, "Ride, Sally Ride." Others cheered. Many women leaders were among the crowd as Sally Ride roared into space.

1986	**1987**	**1996**
Investigates the Challenger *accident; writes* To Space & Back	*Leaves* **NASA***; begins teaching at Stanford University*	*Begins EarthKAM; made a member of the Astronaut Hall of Fame*

Faraway Places

Sally Kristen Ride was born on May 26, 1951, in Encino, California. Her father, Dr. Dale Ride, taught **political science** at Santa Monica College. Sally's mother, Joyce, had been a teacher.

When Sally was young, her mother helped students from other countries learn English. Sally and her sister, Karen, enjoyed learning about faraway places.

When Sally was nine and Karen was seven, their father took them to Europe.

This is a picture of Sally and her younger sister Karen.

This map shows Encino, California, where Sally Ride was born, and Europe, where she traveled with her family at the age of nine.

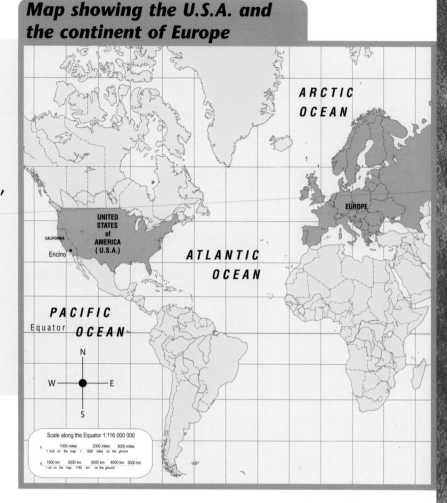

Map showing the U.S.A. and the continent of Europe

ARCTIC OCEAN

EUROPE

UNITED STATES of AMERICA (U.S.A.)

CALIFORNIA

Encino

ATLANTIC OCEAN

PACIFIC OCEAN

Equator

N
W   E
S

Scale along the Equator 1:116 000 000

0   1000 miles   2000 miles   3000 miles
1 inch on the map = 1830 miles on the ground

0   1000 km   2000 km   3000 km   4000 km   5000 km
1 cm on the map 1160 km on the ground

The family spent an entire year traveling. Sally did not attend school. Her parents thought she should be able to explore the world around her. The Rides visited many cities in Europe and hiked through the countryside. Sally loved exploring. She dreamed that one day she would be among the brave explorers to travel to outer space.

Early Interests

Sally always loved sports. She played soccer, baseball, and football with children in her neighborhood. She learned to read by the age of five. She read mysteries, adventure stories about space travel, and the sports pages of the newspaper. She was a good student.

When she returned from the year in Europe, Sally skipped a grade in school. She also began playing tennis. She loved the game and practiced for hours.

This woman is about to serve in tennis, the sport Sally loved.

Sally is fifth from the right in this photo of the tennis team of the Westlake School for Girls.

When she was eleven years old, Sally took lessons from Alice Marble, who had been a great tennis player. Sally played in junior competitions. She won a partial **scholarship** to a private high school, The Westlake School for Girls, because of her tennis playing and her good grades. She was ranked the eighteenth junior tennis player in the country. For a while Sally thought she might earn her living as a tennis player.

Star Student

As a junior in high school, Sally discovered that she liked science. Her teacher, Dr. Elizabeth Mommaerts, gave Sally special projects and helped her develop her interest in science. After she **graduated** from Westlake School, Sally went to Swarthmore College in Pennsylvania. Sally missed California, where she could play tennis all year. After a year and a half, she went home, but soon realized that she would never be a **champion** tennis player.

Sally studied at Swarthmore College for a year and a half.

William Shakespeare lived 400 years ago, but people still enjoy his plays.

When Sally returned to school at Stanford University in California, she studied **physics,** the science of energy and matter. As a graduate student, Sally majored in astrophysics, the study of energy process in stars and galaxies. In her English class, Sally read the plays of William Shakespeare, a writer who lived in the 1600s. For Sally, reading Shakespeare was like doing puzzles, looking for clues to find meaning. Sally earned two degrees, one in physics and one in English.

Reaching for the Stars

After getting her college degree, Sally stayed at Stanford and continued to study for her Master's degree. At Stanford, Sally studied the X rays, invisible waves of energy, given off by stars. Her days were spent doing research and helping to teach younger students. Sally wondered what to do next. One day while reading the student newspaper, she saw an advertisement for astronauts. **NASA** was looking for scientists, engineers, and doctors to perform experiments on space shuttle missions. The ad said that women would be welcome to apply. Sally was one of over 8,000 people who applied.

Scientists use telescopes to see stars like the ones in this photograph.

The Johnson Space Center is the home base for astronauts.

While she waited to hear from NASA, Sally received another degree from Stanford. She was now Dr. Ride.

In October 1977, Dr. Ride went to the Johnson Space Center in Houston, Texas, for interviews and tests. Four months later, on January 16, 1978, she got a phone call from NASA. She was one of six women who had been chosen to train as astronauts. The women shared a curiosity about space. They soon became friends.

Flying Lessons

The first women astronauts are shown here together.
Sally Ride is the one on the far left.

During astronaut training, Dr. Ride studied **meteorology, astronomy,** computers, and mathematics. She worked 60 hours a week learning the parts of the space shuttle and how it worked. She practiced parachute jumping and learned how to survive in the wilderness so she would be prepared for emergencies. Dr. Ride spent several hours a week in a T-38 jet learning how pilots use the radios and navigate, or find their way, while flying.

Satellites

Satellites help us in many ways. For example, some satellites send radio and television signals to Earth. Others predict the weather.

Dr. Ride liked flying so much that she took lessons and earned an airplane pilot's license. In August 1979, she finished her first year of astronaut training. While she waited to go into space, Dr. Ride continued to study the space shuttle. She helped scientists in Canada develop a robot arm for the shuttle. The arm would be used to lift **satellites** into and out of the shuttle's **cargo bay.**

Ride is shown here learning how to use firefighting equipment.

Famous Firsts

When the shuttle went into space for the second and third times, Dr. Ride worked as the **capcom,** or capsule communicator. She was the only person on Earth who talked with the shuttle crew while they were in space. Dr. Ride gave the astronauts the information they needed from the experts at **NASA** and passed along their reply. She was the first woman to serve as a capcom. People wondered if Sally would be the first American woman to go into space.

This is a picture of the first shuttle landing. Behind the shuttle is a chase plane. Ride often rode in chase planes.

As capcom, Ride talked to the astronauts on the shuttle.

In April 1982, NASA announced that Dr. Sally Ride would be a mission specialist on the next shuttle flight. She was chosen because she could work well with the robot arm and with the other astronauts.

First Women in Space

*On June 16, 1963, Russian **cosmonaut** Valentina Tereshkova was the first woman in space. On August 19, 1982, cosmonaut Svetlana Savitskaya became the second woman in space when she flew to the Salyut 7 space station. Sally Ride would be the third woman in space.*

Getting Ready to Fly

Dr. Ride was excited. At last her dream of going into space would come true. Reporters asked a lot of questions. They wanted to know what Dr. Ride would wear. She told them that she would wear the same flight suit as the men wore. She tried to talk about the shuttle mission, the crew, and the science of the trip, but the reporters kept asking her how it felt to be the first American woman in space.

Ride's Firsts

Sally Ride was the first American woman to:

- *serve as **capcom***
- *go into space*
- *take a second flight*
- *become a member of the Astronaut Hall of Fame.*

In this picture the STS-7 crew Ride is sitting to commande Robert Crippe

18

Ride and pilot Frederick Hauck practiced using the robot arm.

Training for the shuttle mission took all of Dr. Ride's time. She spent many hours in the **simulator,** and she practiced using the robot arm she had helped to design. Dr. Ride and astronaut John Fabian would use the arm to put a **satellite** into orbit. Dr. Ride would also help the shuttle pilot during takeoff and landing. If a problem occurred, she was ready to help.

Into Space

At 3:15 A.M. on Saturday, June 18, 1983, the shuttle crew woke up, got dressed, and ate breakfast. They took a van to the Florida launch pad and rode an elevator up 30 stories to the space shuttle. They climbed into the space shuttle, checked the instruments, and waited. At 7:33 A.M. the shuttle roared into space.

Seconds later, Sally saw the shuttle zoom past clouds. It took eight-and-a-half minutes for the shuttle to reach outer space.

The space shuttle *Challenger* is slowly rolled to the launch for its flight into space.

From space, Ride talks to NASA scientists on the ground. She is holding a tape recorder.

Mission Specialist

Mission specialist *is NASA's name for scientists who are astronauts.*

Dr. Ride enjoyed every minute of the flight. Without **gravity** to hold her feet to the ground, she floated around the shuttle and looked at Earth from space. As a mission specialist, she helped with several experiments and worked the big robot arm to move **satellites** into and out of the shuttle's **cargo bay**.

Back to Earth

Because of rain storms in Florida, the shuttle landed at Edwards Air Force Base in California.

Most of Dr. Ride's time on the shuttle was spent working on the experiments. She also studied stars outside the shuttle windows and took photographs. Dr. Ride loved being **weightless.** Before the astronauts left Earth, President Ronald Reagan sent them a package of jelly beans to take on their journey. During the flight, they tossed the weightless jelly beans across the cabin and tried to catch them in their mouths. The trip ended after six days in space.

The shuttle returned to Earth on June 24, 1983. President Reagan called the crew to welcome them home. Everyone wanted to talk to Dr. Ride about her trip into space. She understood that people were curious about the first American woman in space. She gave her space suit to the Smithsonian Institution's National Air and Space Museum, and she talked about space travel on *Sesame Street*.

Ride joined *Sesame Street*'s Grundgetta to teach children about the letter "A" for *astronaut*.

Flight Problems

On October 5, 1984, Dr. Ride took her second trip into space aboard the *Challenger*. Dr. Ride worked with the robot arm again and studied Earth from space using special cameras and equipment. The crew included one of Dr. Ride's childhood classmates, Kathryn Sullivan, who became the first woman to walk in space during the flight. There were several equipment problems on the flight, and Dr. Ride worked hard to solve them.

Ride and astronaut Kathryn Sullivan used velcro and cords to hold their sleeping bags in place during space flight.

Ride watched from the ground as the space shuttle *Challenger* exploded 73 seconds after liftoff.

Dr. Ride's third mission was planned for July 1986, but she never went. She was in training for her mission when the space shuttle *Challenger* exploded during its January 1986 flight. Dr. Ride knew the astronauts who were killed on that flight. Like other Americans, she was shocked and upset. But Dr. Ride was a scientist and an astronaut, and she wanted to help. When President Reagan asked her to help look into the cause of the *Challenger* accident, she agreed.

Investigations

The *Challenger* crew who died when the shuttle exploded were (front row, from left) Mike Smith, Dick Scobee, Ron McNair, (back row, from left) Ellison Onizuka, Sharon Christa McAuliffe, Greg Jarvis, and Judy Resnik.

Dr. Ride worked with twelve other experts to find the answer. They discovered that in the cold weather a seal, called an O ring, had failed to work on the booster rocket, the engine used to control the shuttle in space. They told **NASA** how to fix the problem.

In 1986 Dr. Ride finished writing a book for children about her journey into space.

The book is called *To Space and Back*. It includes photographs taken by the astronauts. Dr. Ride hoped it would teach children about space flight.

NASA asked Dr. Ride to work at their Washington, D.C., office. She wrote a report about the United States space program which became known as *The Ride Report*. She recommended that NASA put humans on the Moon, on space stations, and on Mars.

Dr. Ride left NASA in 1987 on her 36th birthday. She moved to California and began teaching **physics** at Stanford University. Two years later, she moved to the University of California at San Diego.

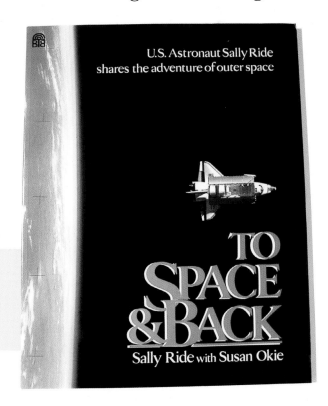

This book by Sally Ride is filled with pictures taken from space.

Planning for the Future

In 2001 Dr. Ride began a group called Imaginary Lines to help girls develop their interest in science, math, and **technology**. Imaginary Lines runs science festivals and science camps for sixth- to ninth-grade girls.

On February 1, 2003, the space shuttle *Columbia* exploded as it reentered Earth's atmosphere. President George W. Bush asked Dr. Ride to work with a group of people to study the cause of the crash. As a scientist, she was able to help solve the problem so that space missions can continue.

Anyone can visit the Sally Ride Science Club website and learn about science.

Ride smiled when she joined the Astronaut Hall of Fame on June 21, 2003.

Sally Ride said:

"We need kids to look to the stars. It's science, technology, and engineering that really drive our country forward and make it a better place."

Dr. Ride teaches **physics** to college students, does research on **lasers,** and supports children who want to study science. Imaginary Lines continues to help girls to focus on science and math. So does the Sally Ride Science Club. Dr. Ride is in charge of EarthKAM, a project that allows students to take pictures from a camera on the *International Space Station.* When she imagines the future, Dr. Ride sees a world where boys and girls will be able to explore the far reaches of outer space.

Glossary

astronomy   study of the stars

capcom   person who talks to the crew during shuttle mission

cargo bay   open area of shuttle which can open and close and is used to hold satellites and science equipment

cosmonaut   Russian astronaut

graduate   complete school

gravity   force that draws things toward Earth

laser   device that creates a powerful beam of light

meteorology study of weather

Mission Control   NASA experts who help run the space mission

NASA   National Aeronautics and Space Administration, the agency that studies and carries out work in space

physics   science that studies energy and matter

political science   study of government

satellite   object which goes around another object in space

scholarship   money to help pay for education

simulator   model of a space vehicle used in training

technology   inventions that improve our lives

weightless   having little or no weight due to lack of gravity in space

More Books to Read

Ride, Sally, with Susan Okie. *To Space and Back*. New York: Lothrop, Lee & Shepard, 1986.

Ride, Sally and Tam O'Shaughnessy. *The Third Planet: Exploring the Earth from Space*. New York: Crown, 1994.

Ride, Sally and Tam O'Shaughnessy. *The Mystery of Mars*. New York: Crown, 1999.

Ride, Sally and Tam O'Shaughnessy. *Exploring Our Solar System*. New York: Crown, 2003.

Places to Visit

Kids Space Place
Space Center Houston
1601 NASA Parkway (formerly NASA Rd 1)
Houston, Texas 77058
Visitor Information: (281) 244-2100

Kennedy Space Center Visitor Complex
Route 405
Orsino, Florida 32899
Visitor information: (321) 449-4444

Index